TRULY MONST[...]

Vampires

TRULY MONSTROUS TALES

Vampires

Peter Hepplewhite & Neil Tonge

Illustrated by Anne Curtis

Hodder
Children's
Books

a division of Hodder Headline plc

Text copyright © 1999 Peter Hepplewhite & Neil Tonge
Illustrations copyright © 1999 Anne Curtis
Published by Hodder Children's Books1999

Design by Linda Reed & Associates

A catalogue record for this book is available from the British Library

ISBN 0 34073992 4

Printed and bound in Great Britain by The Guernsey Press Company Limited,
Guernsey, C.I.

Hodder Children's Books
a division of Hodder Headline plc
338 Euston Road
London NW1 3B7

Contents

For Joe the biting baby

Introduction

Have you cut or grazed yourself recently? What's the first thing you did – after you yelped? We bet you sucked the wound. Remember the taste, salty, warm and metallic? It's one of the oldest tastes in the world – the taste of life – the taste of blood.

Prehistoric people knew the importance of blood. If someone was injured, they bled. When an animal was hunted and killed, it bled. They knew that drinking fresh blood meant strength while loss of blood meant death. From this knowledge came fear. If people fed on animals, what might feed on people? Across the world, from Ancient Greece to Ancient India and China, legends were told of creatures that thrived on human blood. And worse, this gave them powers to defy death itself. They were 'the undead'. They were vampires!

The modern vampire craze began in 1897 when Bram Stoker's novel *Dracula* was published. Stoker based his horror story on eerie folk tales from Eastern Europe. Brilliantly, he brought his grim creation, Count Dracula, to London. The monster roamed the modern city and chilled the blood of Victorian readers. Van Helsing, the Dutch vampire hunter in Stoker's novel, explains the Count's vast powers:

> *The vampire cannot die by the mere passing of time... He throws no shadow; he makes no reflection in the mirror. He has the strength of many... He can transform himself into a wolf... He can be a bat... He can come in a mist which he creates. He can come on moonlight rays as elemental dust... He can see in the dark.*

How can mere mortals defeat such a supernatural being? This is the fearsome challenge that still makes vampires a sure-fire hit in popular horror stories and films today.

Dare you let this book introduce you to the truly monstrous world of vampires? Inside you'll find coffins stuffed with stories of the 'undead' – from the real Prince Dracula, a killer far worse than any vampire – to the dreadful Chupacabras of Puerto Rico, a bloodsucker with a fatal love of goats. Read on and if a vampire knocks on your door you'll know what to do. Sharpened stake ready? OK... start reading.

Peter and *Neil*

Dracula, the Dark Prince

Do you believe in Dracula, the prince of darkness? No? Well you ought to. Dracula was a *real person*... and far more terrible than any supernatural monster. In the 15th century he was the prince of a country called Wallachia, now part of Romania. For most of his reign he was a bloody tyrant feared by his own people, yet for one year he became an unlikely hero in the fight against the mighty Turkish empire.

The Night of Terror

On the night of June 17, 1462 Dracula was fighting for his life. Angrily he slashed at the face of a Turkish soldier. The man clutched his head and fell but two more guards rushed forward to take his place. Dracula cursed. No matter how many Turks he killed, he was always outnumbered.

Dracula had led his tiny army on a last desperate attack. The plan was simple and brutal: hit the vast enemy camp hard and fast, kill the Sultan* and escape. Dracula's horse whinnied and reared, hooves glinting in the scattered light of the camp fires. His men screamed like demons behind him as they charged towards the Sultan's pavilion. If fate was on his side, the next few minutes would make him the most famous warrior in the world. If not, his reign was over...

Sultan: the ruler of the Turkish Empire.

The Turks Attack

The threat from Turkey had been looming for years. The Turks were fierce soldiers of Islam who had conquered most of the Middle East. In 1453, led by Sultan Mehmed II they had captured the fabulous city of Constantinople. Mehmed made it the capital of his growing Muslim empire and renamed it Istanbul. From this new base Mehmed struck again in 1458 and took over Greece.

Christians everywhere felt a shudder of fear: the Turks were merciless to those who refused to become Muslims. In 1459, Pope Pius II, leader of the Catholic Church, pleaded for 100,000 gold ducats* to fight a crusade, a holy war, against the heathen* hordes. But the kings of Europe were not listening. They had their own petty squabbles and they prayed the Turks would leave them alone. Only one monarch came forward to fight – Dracula, Prince of Wallachia. The Prince cared little for religion but he saw that for the time being his interests and those of the Pope were the same – getting rid of the Turks.

Dracula knew the Turks better than most. His father, Dracul, had been a member of the Order of the Dragon, a band of kings and knights, sworn to fight the Muslim enemy. In 1443, when he was 12 years old, Dracula and his brother, Radu the Handsome, had been captured by the Turks. They were held as hostages for five years to make sure their father obeyed the Sultan. During his time as a prisoner young Dracula had even served in the Turkish army, learning how to fight like a Turk. Sadly for his country he had also learned never to trust anyone – and never to forgive or forget those who crossed him. Even his guards came to fear him.

Dracula Declares War

Dracula was crowned Prince Vlad IV of Wallachia in June 1456. His tiny country was on the edge of the Turkish empire and to stay at peace with his powerful neighbour

---

Ducats: valuable gold coins.
Heathen: an insulting term for people who were not
Christian.

he paid a tax. This wasn't simply a tax of gold or silver, but of children! Every year, 500 Wallachian boys were handed over to the Turkish army. After a long and brutal training they became janissaries, the most deadly of all the Sultan's soldiers.

By paying this terrible tax Dracula was buying time. For years he had been busy killing thousands of his own subjects whom he suspected were plotting against him. (For this grisly story turn to page 22.) But by the autumn of 1461 Dracula felt safe enough at home to strike at enemies abroad. Now, according to a Russian story, he threw down a challenge to the Turks that they could not afford to ignore. He stopped paying his taxes.

As Dracula expected, the Sultan sent ambassadors to find out why the Wallachian payments were late. The ambassadors entered Dracula's palace and bowed politely but refused to take off their turbans. Dracula was furious – removing hats was a mark of respect in Europe. He demanded, "Why do you behave like this in front of me. You are ambassadors from the great court at Istanbul. Do you think Turkish envoys are better than Christian kings? Have you been sent to shame me?"

"My Lord," they quickly explained, "we are only following the customs of our homeland. We do not remove our hats – even in front of the Sultan." Smiling cruelly, Dracula told them, "Then I am only too pleased to help you keep your ways. Let us test Turkish courage."

With a sweep of his hand he ordered the turbans to be nailed to their heads. The shocked and bleeding envoys were sent back to the Sultan with a blunt message.

Tell Mehmed II not to force his customs on other rulers who do not want them.

This was a declaration of war.

In the first months of fighting, Dracula's troops overran Bulgaria and smashed the Turks. Dracula claimed that 23,884 people were killed, 'without counting those whom we burned in their homes or those who did not have their heads cut off by my men.' He pushed on and reached the coast of the Black Sea, causing panic amongst the enemy. Across Europe Dracula was hailed as a hero, and church bells were rung from Genoa to Paris to celebrate his victories. But, as winter thawed into the spring of 1462, Dracula's luck ran out.

Dracula's Retreat

Mehmed II himself led a new Turkish army to crush the upstart Prince of Wallachia. For days the Sultan's countless troops crossed the Straits of the Bosphorus on a fleet of barges. As the odds mounted against him, Dracula begged for reinforcements from other Christian kings – yet no one sent help. Realising that his kingdom stood alone, Dracula prepared for a bitter, fighting retreat. He intended to turn his country into a desert rather than surrender.

When the Turks advanced into Wallachia a few weeks later they found a devastated land. Dracula had ordered his people to escape into the mountains and forests or join the army. Before fleeing they had set fire to their homes, leaving only ruined ghost towns. Nothing was left that could be useful to the invaders – crops were burned, wells poisoned, animals slaughtered and rivers dammed to make impassable marshes. The weather, too, seemed to be on the side of Wallachia. There was a scorching summer in 1462 and to the weary Turkish soldiers it seemed as if their burning armour would melt like candle wax. Soon the Turks were desperate for water and even the best scouts had to search for miles to seek out springs that had not been poisoned.

In spite of this, Dracula knew his small army would lose a pitched battle with the Sultan's hordes. The best he could hope for was to unnerve Mehmed with his ferocity. Again and again he stung the Turks with hit-and-run attacks. Since Dracula's troops knew the lie of the land they seemed to be everywhere. His cavalry sprang from hidden paths to kill stragglers or ambush messengers and supply wagons. Pits were dug and covered with branches and leaves to trap men, camels and horses. If prisoners were taken they suffered a terrible torture – impalement. They were cruelly stuck on pointed stakes, and left to die.

Even the very sick and criminals had to fight. Men with deadly diseases such as leprosy, tuberculosis, smallpox and the plague were dressed as Turks and sent to infect the enemy camp. Murderers were released from prison and promised their freedom if they brought back the head of an invader. But Mehmed was equally tough. Ignoring their losses, slowly and unstoppably the Turks closed in on the helpless Wallachian capital city, Tirgoviste.

The Last Gamble

Staring defeat in the face, Dracula planned a last gamble – a battle the Turks came to call the Night of Terror. On that dark June night Dracula led his cavalry on a desperate raid to kill the Sultan. As the sun dipped, the vast Turkish camp settled into the usual routine. Watchful guards patrolled the perimeter; the tempting smell of roast lamb drifted through the air; Christian slaves, thinking of their homes, cried softly; bad-tempered camels brayed and spat; women visitors to the royal court laughed quietly, hoping to catch the eye of the Sultan. In the centre of all this activity, protected by his janissaries, stood the proud, golden tent of Mehmed II. Inside the Sultan had gone sleepily to bed after a large meal.

From the dense forest nearby came the eerie hoot of an owl. The guards ignored the mournful call but this was the signal Dracula's men had been waiting for. Attack! Suddenly the night exploded with the drumming of hoof beats. The Turkish guards were cut down as the Wallachians burst into their camp. A few cried out a warning as they died: 'Kaziklu Bey' – 'the Impaler'.

Like a flash flood Dracula's cavalry hacked their way forward. Dazed Turkish soldiers were butchered as they sat by their camp fires or staggered sleepily from their tents. Wallachian swords and lances ran red with the blood of thousands. Yet, as trumpets sounded the alarm, the Turks slowly began to fight back. By the time Dracula came in sight of the Sultan's pavilion he knew his wager had failed. Between him and his victim stood fierce rows of janissaries, men who would die to save their Master.

Realising that his force was in danger of being wiped out, Dracula gave the order to retreat. But the escape from the Turkish camp was not like the glorious charge that carried the Wallachians in. Hundreds of his precious men were dragged down and killed as they struggled to break out. Worse, the Sultan had survived. In the thin dawn light Dracula knew he had no choice but to burn his own city of Tirgoviste.

When the Turks came in sight of Dracula's capital they found the gates open for them. But they did not make a triumphal entry. A pall of smoke hung over the city. Holy relics and treasures had been moved or hidden and the wells poisoned. Disappointed and angry, Mehmed turned his army aside to chase after Dracula. Just a few miles to the north however the Turks moved into a narrow gorge and found the blackest horror. The steep sides were lined with impaled corpses – over 20,000 mangled bodies. Many had rotted and birds nested in their bones. Most of the bodies were Wallachians, victims of Dracula's cruelty, but others were fresh – the remains of Turkish prisoners.

For the first time Mehmed sensed the total ruthlessness of Dracula and lost heart. Mehmed ordered his army to turn east and leave this accursed land. But the Sultan was too clever to be beaten by simple brute terror. What he could not win by war, he would win by cunning. He sent for Radu the Handsome and promised to help him take the throne of Wallachia from his elder brother. It was a master stroke. Many Wallachians hated Dracula's cruelty and only fought for him because they hated the Turks more. They flocked to Radu's side and in the coming months drove Dracula out. The evil prince became a fugitive, hiding from his own people in the mountains.

Fang Files

Dracula – a Name to Fear

Dracula's real name was Vlad, like his father. In 1431, Vlad the elder joined the Order of the Dragon and earned the right to carry a flag with a dragon symbol into battle. When they saw this the superstitious peasants of Wallachia nicknamed their prince Dracul – the 'dragon' or the 'devil'.

Vlad the younger had two nicknames. The first, Dracula, was given because of his father. It means the 'son of the dragon' or the 'son of the devil'. The second, Vlad Tepes (said tsep-pesh), he earned with years of horrific treatment of his people. It means Vlad the Impaler.

Bram Stoker based his novel *Dracula* on the ferocious real-life Vlad Tepes and turned him into a blood-sucking vampire. Stoker had done careful research for his evil character. The vampire-hunter Dr Abraham Van Helsing explains:

He must indeed have been that Dracula who won his name against the Turk. If that be so he was no common man; for in that time, and for centuries after, he was spoken of as the cleverest and most cunning, as well as the bravest. That mighty brain and that iron resolution went with him into the grave, and are even now arrayed against us.

Where was Dracula country?

Dracula lived in what is now Romania, but in the 15th century this part of Europe, the Balkans, was a jigsaw puzzle of smaller countries. In his novel, Bram Stoker set the Dracula story in Transylvania. This is only partly true. Dracula was born in Transylvania and lived there at different times of his life. The land he ruled, however, was across the border, the blood-soaked kingdom of Wallachia.

Dracula the Evil Prince

If Dracula was a hero briefly in 1461, what had he done in the years before that made his people fear and hate him? The list is endless. He was a ruthless and ready to do anything to keep his throne. It was the bloodthirsty stories about Vlad Tepes that made him such an attractive villain for Bram Stoker. You may need a friend in the room before you read this catalogue of horror. *Dracula you are accused of:*

Slaughtering the Nobles

When Dracula became Prince in 1456 he wanted revenge against the enemies of his family. His father, Dracul, and his eldest brother, Mircea, had been assassinated in 1447. Mircea's death had been grisly – blinded with red-hot pokers and buried alive. The murderers were Wallachian nobles, called *boyars* in Romanian.

To celebrate his reign, Dracula, invited hundreds of boyars to a meeting in the hall of his palace at Tirgoviste. They were rich and confident men, used to treating princes as tools in their own power games. As Dracula looked at the false smiles of his guests he knew that his father's and brother's killers were among them. Quietly he flattered the crowd:

"You are my most loyal subjects. Tell me how many princes have reigned over our small country during your long lives."

Some of the audience laughed and chuckled. They had not seen the danger in the question.

"Seven, my Lord," shouted one boyar

"I have lived through 30 reigns," said an old grey beard proudly.

"Since your grandfather's time, my liege, there have been no less than 20 princes. I have out lived them all," called another.

Now, sniggering at Dracula, each boyar yelled out an answer, like a class of rude children to a new teacher. They were testing their prince and he saw the challenge. His eyes flickered angrily and he barked out orders. The hall was surrounded by soldiers from his personal bodyguard and over 500 boyars, together with their wives and families, were arrested. They were dragged outside and impaled as fast as the stakes could be cut. Their bodies were left to moulder outside the palace – a warning that Vlad Tepes was here to stay.

Brutality to the Germans

Many rich German merchants and traders lived in Transylvania. Dracula was born in Schassburg, one of their towns, but this didn't earn them any favours. He feared they might help one of his remaining brothers steal his kingdom and decided to teach them who was boss. He rounded up over 400 young Germans working in Wallachia and burned them to death.

Yet this was only the start. In 1460 he led an army of 20,000 against the German towns. During the raid he tortured and killed over 10,000 people. The city of Brasov was captured and St Bartholomew's church burned and robbed. The hills around were grimly decorated with hundreds of prisoners impaled on stakes. In the hot summer sun their bodies began to rot...

Murdering the Noble with the Refined Nose

Not a good place for a picnic you might think, but Dracula had other ideas. He was keen to show his power and what could be better than a banquet to be laid out amongst the pitiful German corpses? His unwilling dinner guests were the boyars in his own army. Dracula knew that the more they saw with their own eyes how he punished his foes, the more likely they were to obey orders. One noble, more stupid or brave than the others, complained. Holding his nose with disgust he pointed out that the bad smell might cause diseases.

Dracula snapped back, "Do you mean to say it stinks here? Servants, bring me a stake three times as long as the ones used on the Germans. And you, my friend, you shall go on the end of it, so high up the stink can't offend your delicate nose."

The noble fell to his knees and frantically kissed Dracula's hand. "Please my lord," he begged. "I meant no offence." But his words fell on deaf ears. A few minutes later he was impaled.

Tricking the Turks

One old Russian story hints that Dracula won his first battles against the Turks in 1461 by using trickery. The tale goes that the Sultan sent one more ambassador to demand his taxes from Wallachia. This time Dracula didn't nail the envoy's turban to his head, far from it – he feasted and flattered him.

Dracula spoke lovingly of the Sultan. "Tell my Master," he purred, "I not only want to pay the tribute but I'll put my whole army at his service. I shall obey his commands and I shall come personally and bow before him. But first let him promise that no harm shall come to me or my men as we travel through his empire."

The Sultan was delighted. He was fighting a war in the East and wanted peace on his Western border. At once he sent a message to all his fortified cities that they should welcome Dracula.

For five days the Prince of Wallachia led his army through Turkish lands, cheered and feasted by the Sultan's subjects. Then he attacked. Turning back the way they had come, the Wallachians fell with savage surprise on the unwary Turkish towns. Thousands of Muslim prisoners were taken and impaled, burned or cut in two. Not even babies were spared.

Gleefully Dracula sent another message to the Turkish leader. "Tell the Sultan I have served him well. If this has pleased him I am ready to do the same again with all my might."

Cruelty to the Army

As you have read, Dracula had a lucky escape from the Turkish camp on the Night of Terror. Yet this didn't change his character. After the raid he inspected the troops who had survived the forlorn attack. He picked out those soldiers who had a wound on the front of their bodies and gave them a generous reward. He made them knights and presented them with fine, new weapons. But those who had a wound in the back were dragged to the front and knocked to their knees. "You are cowards. You are not men, only old women," he screamed at them. Within minutes they had all been impaled as a warning to the others. Now no one could doubt that in Dracula's army it was better to die than run away.

Upholding the Law

Dracula hated thieves, robbers and crooks of all kinds and if any were caught breaking his laws, they could expect a nasty death. A Romanian story tells us that one benefit of Dracula's harsh rule was that Wallachia was almost crime-free. To prove this he had a solid gold cup placed by a drinking fountain next to a busy highway. It was used every day by dozens of travellers from many different countries, but was never stolen.

Rough Justice for a Merchant

Russian and Romanian tales tell of the merchant who visited Dracula's court at Tirgoviste. Some say he was a Hungarian, others that he was from Florence in Italy. He was travelling through Wallachia with a treasure chest of gold and a wagon load of valuable goods. Nervous in case he was robbed, the merchant asked Dracula for guards to protect his valuables overnight. To his dismay the Prince not only denied his request but commanded him to park his wagon in a public square in a dark and poor area of the city. Worse, Dracula invited him and his servants to stay the night in the palace – far from the wagon. It was an invitation that couldn't be refused.

After a sleepless night the poor man ran to the square only to find that his gold, a fortune of 160 ducats, had gone. Dracula seethed with fury. He ordered that Tirgoviste be turned upside-down to find the culprit, and he sent out a stark message to the people, "Give me this thief or I will burn your homes."

That night he had the merchant's gold replaced from his own treasury – together with a crafty trap. The next morning the merchant was overjoyed to find the ducats and counted them eagerly – once (Was there a mistake?), twice (No, there was not a mistake), three times (Perhaps he had better be honest in this barbaric court). "Sire," the merchant said to Dracula, "My gold has been returned, but strangely there is too much. There are 161 ducats."

At that moment the guards brought in the thief and with him the merchant's original gold. As you might expect, justice was swift and brutal – the thief was impaled. The merchant looked on, puzzled, until Dracula explained.

"You have passed my little test. If you had not confessed that there was too much money you would have joined the thief in his last dance of agony. Now you may go in peace and keep the extra ducat for your honesty."

What happened to Dracula?

After he fled Wallachia in 1462, Dracula turned for help to his neighbour, King Matthias of Hungary. Yet, far from being welcomed, he was arrested and imprisoned. Matthias claimed he had letters to prove that Dracula had offered to fight alongside the Turks in an attack on Hungary.

Although this kind of treachery was typical of Dracula, most historians think that in this case he was framed. Matthias had forged the letters and was playing his own crooked games. Matthias had been given a fortune by the Pope to send an army to help Dracula. Remember, for a little while in 1461 many people across Europe thought Dracula was a good guy fighting the terrible Turks. The letters, however, gave Matthias the perfect excuse to do nothing – and hang on to the money. Well it was tough luck on Dracula, but can you really feel sorry for him??

From 1462 until 1474 Dracula was held under house arrest in Hungary. Being locked up didn't improve his character. Russian stories claim that since he couldn't torture people he started picking on birds and mice. When war broke out between Hungary and Turkey, Matthias brought Dracula out of his forced retirement. In 1476, he was made Prince of Wallachia again and died fighting against the Turks. Dracula and his personal bodyguard of 200 fought to the last man, surrounded by a wall of Turkish corpses. His head was sent as a trophy to the Sultan in Constantinople – proof that the ferocious impaler was finally dead.

Have you heard the phrase, trouble runs in families? A hundred years after his death a distant relative of Dracula's went on a killing spree in Hungary. Can your trembling fingers turn the pages to find out all about the Bloody Countess..?

The Bloody Countess

The King's Plot

HUNGARY, 1610

King Matthias II of Hungary listened eagerly to the report. The news was all he could have hoped for. "At last," he yelled gleefully to his secretary, "The Bathory witch has gone too far. Now I can get her."

The King turned over the facts of the thorny case in his mind. Countess Elizabeth Bathory had been murdering peasant girls for years and Matthias had long wanted to arrest her, but politics left him powerless. The victims were only simple country folk and worth less to the nobles who owned them than a good horse. And then there were the Bathorys to consider. Elizabeth's family was amongst the greatest in Hungary, and the King had foolishly borrowed a fortune from the Countess herself. If the King tried to uphold the law the Bathory clan would claim he was using the murders as an excuse to cheat on his debts. The Bathorys would rebel and other nobles, keen to see that the King did not get too strong, would join in. All in all, a tricky situation. At least it had been until now!

Thankfully the report was clear. Elizabeth had enticed the daughter of a wealthy neighbour to her castle and killed her. The Countess claimed it was suicide, but the girl's terrible wounds proved the story a lie. The victim's family was not as powerful as the Bathorys but they were nobles – and they demanded action. This time the killings couldn't be ignored.

The King grinned. If he handled the situation well he would come out of it very nicely. The peasants had muttered fearfully for years about Elizabeth being a vampire – a demon in league with the Devil. If royal officials could prove this to a court of law, Elizabeth would be condemned to death as a witch. A verdict of guilty meant the King could confiscate her land, wipe out all of his debts and get rid of the Bloody Countess once and for all.

Count Thurzo's Plot

A few days later, Matthias travelled to Bratislava, a large town near Elizabeth's castle at Cachtice. He summoned the local Governor, Count Gyorgy Thurzo, and told him his plans. The King ordered Thurzo to investigate and come back with hard evidence to prove witchcraft and murder. Bowing low, Thurzo agreed, but while his face was masked with a smile he was already scheming to cross Matthias.

The King had been careless in his choice of investigator. Thurzo was a friend and kin of the Bathorys. The Count agreed that Elizabeth had to be dealt with, but not in a way that gave Matthias her lands. In a secret meeting he struck a deal with the adult children and closest relatives of the Countess. Elizabeth would be arrested and there would be a quick trial in Thurzo's own castle at Bytca. A local jury would reach a verdict before the King could interfere. Elizabeth would not be allowed to take the stand and most of the blame would be put on her servants.

The Raid

Thurzo raided Castle Cachtice on 29 December, 1610. He chose to attack during the Christmas holidays because much of the royal court would be on holiday and so it would be harder for Matthias to meddle. The castle was lightly guarded and easily captured, but once inside

even Thurzo's hardened soldiers, used to killing, were sickened. The bodies of several young women were uncovered with the grisly trade mark of the Countess – they were drained of blood. Elizabeth screeched and wailed as she was dragged to Bytca, but she was not really worried. She was a Bathory; no one dared touch her.

The Trial and the History of the Countess

Thurzo knew that he had to move quickly for his plot to work. Elizabeth's trial was held on 2 January, the court packed with peasants and petty officials who would do as he told them. Awkward priests who mumbled about witchcraft were bribed to keep quiet. But, as the witnesses gave their evidence, a hideous story unfolded.

Elizabeth was born in 1560 and had showed signs of madness since she was a child. She had been cruel to animals, killing and maiming them in a way that foreshadowed her brutal treatment of people. She may have picked up her evil habits from notorious relatives. One of her uncles prayed to the Devil, and her brother was a drunk who spent a fortune chasing women.

The Countess had been a wild teenager and was pregnant by a peasant boy at 13. The baby was born in secret and smuggled out of the country to avoid a scandal. The following year Elizabeth was hastily married to Ferenc Nadasdy, the Black Knight. The Nadasdys were another powerful Hungarian family and Ferenc a famous soldier fighting against the Turks. It was an arranged marriage to tie up the two great families. But, to her surprise, Elizabeth fell in love with Ferenc and found they had interests in common – torture and brutality. Sadly, it wasn't a happy marriage for those who had to work for them.

While her husband was away, Elizabeth was in charge of running Castle Cachtice and the lands around it. Ferenc told Elizabeth to rule her household with a firm hand. Servants who neglected their duties were ordered to stand in the courtyard in freezing nights while they were doused with buckets of cold water. In these years, Elizabeth first dabbled in murder and grew to like the sight of blood.

In 1600 Ferenc died. Some witnesses claimed Elizabeth had poisoned him, and others that she was shattered by grief. Whatever the truth, Elizabeth became like a carriage careering down a mountain road – completely out of control and very dangerous. She threw her mother-in-law out of the castle and sent her children to live with relatives.

Elizabeth was now 40 and her good looks were starting to fade. Witnesses claimed that one day the ageing Countess was having her hair combed by a young servant girl. The terrified girl accidentally pulled too hard and Elizabeth spun round and slapped her. The blow was so hard that the girl's lip split and some of the blood spurted on to Elizabeth's hand. As she rubbed it off the Countess noticed that her skin seemed smoother... as if it had taken on the servant's youthfulness. After this she began to bath in the blood of her victims, desperately trying to hold back old age.

Her chief accomplices were an evil gang only too pleased to meet every sick whim of their employer: Thorko, a strong thug who kidnapped or bribed girls and brought them to the castle; Ilona Joo, the family nurse and Anna Darvulia, believed by the local peasants to be a sorceress. During the trial, a register found in Anna's private rooms was produced as evidence. It noted the names of 650 people murdered at Castle Cachtice between 1600 and 1610.

Verdict and Punishment

Elizabeth's accomplices were found guilty and executed. Her own punishment was kept secret, to keep the good name of the Bathory and Nadasdy families. In fact, she was walled up in a small room in her own castle, a room without windows and only a small opening for food and air. There she lingered on for three years until her body was found by a jailer in August 1614. Castle Cachtice was abandoned after her death and slowly fell into ruins.

Thurzo was delighted, his plot had worked perfectly. He had dealt with the troublesome Countess and outsmarted the King. Since Elizabeth was not found guilty of witchcraft, Matthias had no excuse for seizing Bathory lands and still owed the family a fortune. Thurzo smiled: Kings and mad Countesses were best kept in their places.

Fang Files

Was the Bloody Countess a Vampire?

Like Prince Dracula, Elizabeth Bathory was not a traditional blood-sucking vampire. She was a real person with monstrous tastes. The local people were so frightened that they accused her of being a vampire, a demon and a werewolf. However she was guilty of vampirism (behaving like a vampire) – drinking and bathing in the blood of her victims.

Beware the Powers of the Vampire

Eastern Europe, especially Romania, was one of the world's vampire hotspots. Folktales and legends struck fear into the hearts of listeners. Like comic strip superheroes, or rather villains, the stories claimed vampires had amazing powers.

The Undead: Vampires were known as the 'undead'. Their journey to the next world had been interrupted and they were doomed to walk the earth forever. Vampires thrived in their new supernatural lives by drinking the blood of mortal creatures – human blood was the tastiest but animals would do.

Vampire Spotting: Are you from a big family? Then look out! Romanians believed that the seventh son of a seventh son was doomed to become a vampire. So were criminals, illegitimate children and babies born with teeth. And of course anyone who didn't like garlic was definitely dodgy.

Vampire Plague: Vampires spread their kind by sharing blood with their victims. This was not quite as easy as the famous bite on the neck in the movies, they also had to force, trick or persuade their prey to drink vampire blood.

Shapeshifting: If a vampire was cornered or in a difficult spot he or she could shapeshift – switch from animal to human form and back again. Favourite vampire shapes were bats, wolves and dogs. In the Bram Stoker novel, Count Dracula came ashore in Britain at Whitby in the shape of a great black dog.

Dark Flight: In the hours of darkness vampires could fly. Romanians called one kind of vampire the Strigoi – the demon birds of the night.

Altering the Forces of Nature: Vampires could cause bad harvests, stop cows giving milk, spread diseases and even make lovers hate each other. Churches had to be kept locked – if a vampire managed to climb the bell tower he or she could yell out the names of villagers and they would die instantly.

Breaking and Entering: Vampires had super strength and could tear down doors and window shutters. If a house was strongly built they could sneak in through the chimney or even the smallest keyhole.

Vengeful Vampires: Vampires were so annoyed at becoming vampires and so jealous of living humans that they wanted revenge. The first people they killed were their own families – then friends, neighbours and anyone else unlucky enough to cross their path.

Stake Out: Everyone knows that vampires can be killed with a wooden stake. Right?? Well don't be too sure. The villagers of Blau in what is now the Czech Republic got a nasty shock during the 13th century. When a vampire terrorised the village they dug his body up and drove a stake through it. The next night the vampire returned, laughing and waving the stake. He thanked them for giving him a stick to beat off the dogs. The attacks didn't stop until his body was dug up again and burned.

Human Again: If a vampire wasn't hunted down and killed within seven years then he or she could travel to a foreign country and become human again. They could marry and even have children, but the poor mites were damned. When they died they took after the vampire side of the family and became 'undead' like Mum or Dad.

Vampire Fireworks: The Gagauz people of Bulgaria called vampires *oburs*. Oburs made noises like exploding firecrackers and could move heavy objects without touching them, like poltergeists (invisible ghosts who like to mess rooms around). Now that's a really useful fact. Next time your bedroom is in a mess you have the perfect excuse. Blame an obur or a poltergeist.

Vampire Hunters

When Romanian peasants had problems with the 'undead' they sent for a professional vampire hunter. The best were known as *dhampir*. No wonder they were good, they were half vampire! Dhampir were said to be the sons of vampires and gypsy women. A gypsy girl who had a vampire lover was not treated like an outcast, but considered rather lucky. Her sons would be born with the instincts of a dhampir – powers to smell and see invisible vampires.

A dhampir knew how to impress those hiring him. He would sniff the air urgently, pulling faces at the stink – that only he could detect. He would sniff his way through the village until he came close to the source of the smell. At this point, off came his shirt and using the sleeve as a telescope he would seek out the invisible enemy – that only he could see.

With the amazed peasants watching, the dhampir would describe the horrible shape of the vampire and then attack it. After a vicious fight the dhampir would stab or shoot the monster, leaving a pool of visible red blood. Did they have special powers or just special trickery? You decide. Whatever the answer they were convincing; dhampir were still in business in Serbia in the 1950s.

Vampire Alert

Worried about a vampire attack? Think the next door neighbour might have gone batty? No friendly gypsies to call on? You'll find your vampire self defence guide in chapter three.

What? You're too scared to read on! You need help now! OK here's a vampire zapping hint. Borrow a large black dog, like a Labrador, and paint an extra set of white eyes on its forehead. This is guaranteed to terrify the undead.

Drink Blood – it's Good for You

You've all heard it! Eat your vegetables, they'll give you iron / clean your system / make you see in the dark / put hairs on your chest. It's the same with blood. The belief that a drop of the red stuff is vital for life and health is ancient – and still around today. Think of people ordering rare steaks in restuarants and all that blood oozing out of the meat. (Apologies to vegetarians, but what do you expect in a book about vampires??) Here to whet your appetite are a few blood-crazed stories.

The Emperor's Daughter

Annia Galeria Faustina was the daughter of the Roman Emperor Antonius Pius. After her marriage she was so desperate to give birth to a son that she drank the blood of gladiators killed in the arena. Perhaps that was part of the problem – she was drinking the blood of losers.

The Vampire of Paris

Pere Lachaise cemetery in Paris was famous as the burial place of artists and musicians. In 1849, however, it became infamous as the scene of horrible crimes. At night an evil creature was opening the graves and eating parts of the bodies. The police set traps and caught a blond, handsome young army officer, Sergeant Françoise Bertrand. His story became the basis for a novel *The Werewolf of Paris* and the 1935 Hollywood movie *The Werewolf of London*. Look out for it on TV.

Crash Pong Wallop!

Can vampires move with the times? Batty Buster Bamford, aged 27, from Carshalton, England, certainly thought so. After buying a second-hand Ford Escort he was soon at his wits' end. The car was a magnet for accidents – six shunts in a few weeks. Not surprisingly, Buster felt that he was having more than his fair share of bad luck and he reckoned he knew the reason why: the Ford was cursed.

Determined not to be outdone by the supernatural, Buster began to take precautions. In February 1999, he told a reporter: "I bought £5 worth of garlic, crushed up the cloves and rubbed them all over the car from bumper to bumper. I haven't had a crash now for two months. The garlic must have some sort of magical property..."

Poor Buster! The accidents had stopped – but so had his love life. After the garlic treatment he just couldn't persuade girls to go for moonlit rides. I wonder why?!

The Vampire of Myconos

As Darkness Falls

The beautiful Greek island of Myconos is set like a green emerald in the bright blue of the Mediterranean Sea. Carpeted with peaceful olive groves it appears to be the last place on earth where you might come face to face with evil, but Joseph Pitton de Tournefort, a French botanist, did just that. De Tournefort landed on the island in 1700 on his way to the Middle East. He was keenly interested in studying the plants and animals of the island, and the customs of the local people. He had not, however, expected to describe a very 'unnatural' event that terrorised Myconos for several days.

A few days before de Tournefort's arrival, the burial of a particularly troublesome peasant had taken place. The man had been loathed for his quarrelsome nature and cheating. His death, whilst welcomed by many of the islanders, had been sudden and swift – for he had been found murdered on a lonely part of the island. No one knew how it had happened or who had done it. This in itself was unsettling, for many of the islanders believed that the dead would not rest in their graves if they had died in such a mysterious circumstance.

Distant members of his family had mumbled a few prayers over his grave and the man had been buried. Then the villagers got on with their lives but kept watch for any unusual happening. As darkness fell after the man's burial, many villagers glanced nervously from their windows at the lengthening shadows of the evening. Some were convinced they could see shapes melt and

reappear in the evening gloom. Others reached for crucifixes, crossed themselves and prayed that God would protect them. And then, to their horror, they became aware of a shape striding from house to house, violently overthrowing chairs and tables and snuffing out candles with breath that stank.

At first, the more respectable of the islanders who hadn't seen anything laughed at the stories of mischief but, as the assaults began to grow more serious, they, too, became alarmed.

No Rest from Evil

Village life came to a standstill. Solemn masses were said in order to drive out the evil presence which all believed to be that of a vampire. Priests intoned prayers and filled the air with incense. All this effort had no effect. As each night fell, shadows and shapes invaded the village houses. The evening was filled with the noises of unexplained bangs and crashes. No one could sleep for fear of what might happen to them. By the time daylight arrived, the distraught people could scarcely keep awake and dreaded the approach of dusk.

It was in this atmosphere of terror that the leading citizens of the district, along with a number of monks and priests, called a meeting. The place was in uproar. Panic and fear had taken hold and it took all the persuasion of the local priests to prevent the meeting breaking into disorder. "What are we to do?" the villagers demanded of their priests. This was the work of the devil they argued and the priests must know how to deal with it. One of the priests cleared his throat and addressed the mob.

"The body is not at peace. We must take the body from the grave and remove the heart. This is the only way we will be able to cast the devil out."

Now this was a very serious proposal. Once buried, the dead were not meant to be disturbed. But if the priest said it would be all right the villagers were not likely to argue with him.

Destruction of the Vampire

The next day a Mass was sung in the chapel where the body had been buried. At the end of the service, the large flagstone covering the man's body was lifted and the freshly dug earth disturbed once more. The coffin was hauled from the yawning hole and laid on the chapel floor. Everyone craned their heads forward and crossed themselves as the lid was levered off, terrified of what may they might see inside.

The crowd parted to make way for the town butcher who had been chosen to do the grisly work. He fell to his knees and, wielding his boning knife, ripped open the body. His hand disappeared into the chest cavity as he

rummaged around to find the heart. Taking as firm a grip as he could, the butcher tugged at the slippery organ. With one enormous heave, he tore the heart loose and held it aloft to show to the fearful congregation.

The corpse of the peasant was now left with a gaping and stinking cavity. From out of the wound, gases began to escape. When their rotten stench mingled with the incense which the priests had burned during the ceremony the air became so loathsome that breathing was difficult. It also had the effect of fuelling the congregation's imagination. Some cried out aloud that they could see a thick cloud of smoke spewing out of the body and the devil himself appearing in the fumes.

Fear ran like a ripple through the crowd which had gathered outside the church. Cries of "Vroucolacas! Vroucolacas!" (the name given to those who rise from the dead) broke out – half-whispered, half-gasped and always accompanied by the crossing of the breast. Children clutched at their parents' hands for protection.

Back in the church more discoveries appeared to confirm the villagers' worst fears. The butcher swore the body was still warm, other witnesses that the blood was fresh and the peasant must have been feeding off the living during his nightly escapades. Those at the rear of the church spilled out into the street, keen to be the first to pass on these deadly observations. As the stories spread, they grew into more terrifying tales. Not only was the blood and body warm but the limbs, in defiance of death, were still supple and could be moved with ease.

Joseph Pitton de Tournefort and his party had taken up a position close to the body and witnessed all that took place. They tried to limit the panic that was setting in, but this proved impossible. Fear was cascading all around them, made worse by the retching at the stench of the rotting corpse.

The heart was held aloft by the butcher clots of gore running down his arm as he carried it triumphantly though the crowd. "Burn it! Burn the devil's heart!" the mob chorused as they followed the bloody pennant to the sea shore. The crowd, like an angry swarm of bees, headed for the nearest of the fires kept burning on the beach by the fishermen.

With a great flourish, the butcher held the heart above his head and threw it into the middle of the flames. The crowd could not take its eyes from the blackening organ, expecting the devil to appear at any moment, crying out in agonised screams.

No Rest for the Dead

If the islanders thought that was an end to the haunting they were mistaken. Indeed, the violence became worse. It was as if the peasant, angered by the treatment of his corpse, had decided on further revenge. Reports flooded in of mysterious beatings of people and animals, but no culprit could be identified. Doors and windows were torn off their hinges, roofs destroyed and full jugs and bottles of wine emptied. Only the house in which de Tournefort was staying seemed unaffected by the mayhem. By now, the panic had gripped almost everyone. Whole families fled with their beds to sleep in the town square. Every morning brought fresh complaints.

The islanders were puzzled. How could the continued outbreak of disorder be explained? Some voiced the view that the ceremony had been conducted wrongly; that the mass should have been sung AFTER the heart had been taken from the body, not BEFORE. In this way the devil would have been caught and destroyed.

In these circumstances they redoubled their efforts to beg for God's help. Solemn processions took place. Priests went on fasts. Holy water was sprinkled in every household and even into the gaping, decomposing mouth of the old peasant – the *vroucolacas*. The remains of the corpse were stabbed over and over again to destroy the vampire, but nothing seemed to do any real good.

Into the Fires of Myconos

Joseph Pitton de Tournefort managed to persuade the islanders to organise night watches. This helped reduce the number of violent and mysterious incidents. Whilst a few beggars and thieves were caught, which helped to explain some of the disturbances, it did not stop them all.

One day as the villagers were chanting their prayers, an Albanian, who was visiting the island, announced that it was pointless to use the swords of Christians on the corpse as they had been doing.

"Can you not see, poor blind buzzards that you are, that the handles of these swords are in the shape of a cross? This prevents the devil issuing out of the body. Why do you not use the curved blades of Turkish scimitars?"

In their desperation the villagers were keen to try anything, no matter how far-fetched it seemed. The corpse was pierced several times with a scimitar – but the mischief continued.

The situation was becoming so intolerable that the villagers became convinced that only by destroying the remains of the corpse would the haunting come to an end. They decided that the vroucolacas needed to be burned and the ashes scattered. Consequently, a great pyre of pitch and tar was prepared. Little was left of the peasant by this time except shreds of decaying flesh, pierced and ripped by the thrusting of swords. These were gathered together and taken with great ceremony to the fire and then thrown into the heart of the flames. Within seconds they were no more than blackened ashes scattered by the wind.

Joseph Pitton de Tournefort saw the flames flicker from a distance as the islanders laughed and slapped each other on the back. They were congratulating themselves, thinking that the vampire who had come back from the dead, had been finally destroyed. The next day, de Tournefort closed his journal after recording the strange events on the island of Myconos and set sail for the Middle East, leaving behind the island of vampires to its fate.

Self-defence Guide against Vampires

If you had been with Joseph Pitton de Tournefort on his expedition how would you have protected yourself against a vampire visit? No, you can't hide under the blankets, that's just the place the vampire will come looking. Scared? Well, don't worry. Just follow these simple rules and you'll be safe from those blood-sucking fiends.

Garlic   If you've been close to anyone who has been eating garlic you can understand why it is a highly favoured (or even highly flavoured) method of warding off vampires. Garlic is found in nearly all parts of the world and is widely used not only for flavouring food but as a medicine. The plant's strong smell and its use as a medicine may be the reasons for believing that it had the power to drive away the forces of darkness. But be careful – too much and it may also drive away your friends.

Seeds   According to legend, vampires are fascinated by seeds. So, if you sense the power of darkness coming toward you, scatter seeds between yourself and the suspicious shape. Any seeds will do the trick. but the most reliable are grass, mustard, linen, millet, carrot, rice or poppy. And if you feel brave enough, scatter them in the coffin or grave of a suspected vampire. It is said that vampires cannot pass over them without feeling the need to count every one. By that time, dawn will have safely arrived and the next night, the Count will have to start counting again!

Thorns   This is a prickly subject for vampires. They will quickly get the point that they're not welcome if they can be lured into thorn bushes. The use of thorn hedges to protect animals and villagers in the distant past from attack probably suggested this as a means of protection against vampires.

Crucifixes and Holy Water   Throughout Europe, objects sacred to the Christian religion are believed to possess a potent force against evil. Vampires have always been associated with the devil, who naturally finds the symbols and objects of goodness terrifying. Sprinkling holy water on a vampire acts like acid and is guaranteed to dissolve the creature into smoke. Above all, a crucifix will really make him cross!

Fire Vampires find fire just too hot to handle. The use of fire has long been seen as a powerful purifying agent. Burning is the most effective way of cleansing evil from the earth and the firelight can make any pushy vampire a shadow of its former self.

Mirrors and Things Reflect upon this simple idea. Vampires have a particular fear of mirrors. Since they do not have a reflection they are reminded that they are the 'undead' and fly away at the first opportunity. Other little tricks you can try are turning your shoes round to face opposite ways – this confuses the vampire who'll not know which way you went. Pieces of iron or a broom behind the door should sweep away any fear of attack. Best of all, having some silver handy will stop you going 'batty'.

Destroying Vampires

Now, what happens if all these precautions have failed? The next awesome task is to destroy the vampire.

Bullets

A bullet is useful to unsure that a suspected vampire will not even have the chance of roaming around at night. A good old-fashioned broadside fired into the coffin is believed to stop the creature dead with lead. Silver, however, being a pure metal, is slicker.

Decapitation

Cutting off a vampire's head was common folklore throughout Germany and Eastern Europe. When a vampire was suspected of living in the village graveyard, the body was dug up, impaled on a wooden stake and its head hacked off. This grisly operation was meant to stop the vampire using its head to direct the body on its nightly wanderings. The head was then placed between the legs, under the body or, more usually, buried separately. In this way the vampire was given a 'head-start' to hell.

Staking the Vampire

Piercing the heart with a wooden (the wood from the Whitethorn is best) stake is guaranteed to destroy vampires. Sometimes, the clothing of the suspected vampire is nailed to the sides of the coffin and the priest repeats the services for the dead. Often, the body is turned to face downwards before the stake is driven through it. In other cases, it is believed that it need not be the heart that is pierced -- any part of the body can be staked. The important thing to do is prevent the corpse digging deeper into the earth to hide from its enemies and the sunlight.

Village of Fear

A Quiet Life

One of the best-documented and strangest cases of vampirism comes from the little village of Meduegna, near Belgrade, in former Yugoslavia. The details of this terrifying case are contained in a report signed by three army surgeons, a colonel and a lieutenant. These men were all highly reliable members of the army who were not given to superstitious beliefs. Yet what they discovered opened up a terrifying world of the living dead.

In the spring of 1727 a young man called Arnold Paole, who had served as a soldier in the Middle East, returned to his native village of Meduegna. Although he had not been in the army for very long, he had experienced dangerous adventures. His proud boast, as he told the tales of his stunning escapades, was that he had cheated death on many occasions. "Nothing," he said, can kill me."

Now, his fellow villagers were typical peasants and thought that the boastful Paole would come to no good by foolishly challenging fate. However, Paole's boasts were usually made after one or two drinks and the villagers were content to put his behaviour down to 'one too many'.

Paole had managed to return to his village with enough money to buy a cottage and a small plot of land. Here, he was determined to spend the remainder of his days. At first the villagers were a little suspicious that a man so young would want to settle down so early in life. Yet his honesty and steady work habits, despite the occasional drink or two, impressed the villagers and he quickly became a respected member of the community.

A Sense of Unease

Yet there was still a slight oddness in Paole's manner which aroused the suspicion of the villagers. No one could quite put their finger on the reason why they felt uneasy except that Paole seemed to go out of his way to avoid people. Strangest of all, he did everything to avoid meeting Nina, the beautiful daughter of a rich farmer whose land ran alongside that of Paole's. "What a perfect match!" the villagers thought. Wherever small groups of people gathered the women would whisper, "He's a handsome fellow, in good health and with no ties." The men would add, "The two properties joined together would greatly improve the farms. Anyone with one eye can see that!"

Now, Paole could not always avoid meeting Nina as they were close neighbours. As time passed, there was little surprise when it was announced that the two young people were to marry. Yet, even though they were promised to each other in marriage, Nina confessed to her friends that she felt there was still a shadow between them – something in Paole's background that remained unspoken. Nina decided that this obstacle, whatever it was, must be removed. She tackled her fiancé.

"What is troubling you? I love you, yet there is something you have not told me. Unburden your heart, my dear."

A Dreadful Secret

Paole was reluctant but he felt that there must be no secrets between them.

"O Nina, forgive me. I cannot shake loose the feeling that I will die young. When I was in the army I saw such a horrifying spectacle that the memory of it still haunts me. Whilst I was on active service in Greece I was stationed near a spot that had earned a sinister reputation. The people in that part of the world believe that the dead can return from the grave to torment the living. For several nights I was visited by the terrible apparition of a man who had recently died. I could bear it no longer. I went to the grave and uncovered the body, even though it was hallowed ground. I drove a stake through the heart, pulled the corpse from its grave and threw the remains on to a fire. But the memory of what I had done haunted me. I could not stay in that spot any longer, got permission to leave the army and fled back to my village. So far I have escaped any injury but I fear that the vampire I destroyed will seek revenge."

Revenge of the Vampire

Nina tried to comfort Paole, persuading him that he was safe, far from the place where he had been so badly frightened and, for a while, he believed her. They were married and during the following months he knew little else but happiness.

But Paole was still unsettled. As dusk fell each night he could be seen staring into the fading light, watching for moving shadows. Perhaps it was these thoughts that led him to be a little careless; his mind straying back to the bitter memory of his army days. Whatever the cause, the results were fatal.

During the first harvest after his return to the village, Paole was loading hay on to a cart. He climbed the slippery stack to tie a rope around the load but missed his footing and fell to the ground, knocking himself out. He was carried to his bed but, despite the constant care of Nina, he died. Paole was buried in the village churchyard and Nina sobbed her farewells to the husband of her all-too-brief marriage.

The Undead shall not Rest

About a month later, reports started to come in that Paole had been sighted stalking through the village after nightfall. More and more witnesses came forward claiming that they, too, had seen him. They complained that they had been haunted and that, after Paole's nocturnal visits, they had became weak and listless.

Their stories were written down by a team of investigators from the army and entered into an official report. More terrifyingly, a number of these unfortunate souls died shortly afterwards. Panic began to spread throughout the neighbourhood. As the winter nights closed in people were afraid to leave their houses. This did not stop Paole, however, for it was widely believed that his spectre could penetrate closed windows and doors.

Ten weeks after the burial of Paole the villagers held a meeting and decided to dig up the corpse and discover whether he was indeed a vampire. Nina, his widow, was very upset but could do little to alter the firm mood of the villagers. The army authorities were informed and they arrived shortly afterwards to carry out the investigation. Two officers, two army surgeons, a drummer boy who carried the doctor's cases of instruments, the village authorities, the old sexton and his assistants made up the grisly party. Dr Mayo, who was in overall charge takes up the account.

'It was early on a grey morning when the commission visited the quiet cemetery of Meduegna. It is surrounded by a wall of roughly cut stone in the shelter of nearby mountains. Irregularly planted fruit trees dot the landscape. The graves are, for the most part, neatly kept, with borders of tiny box hedges, and flowers between them. Most have a small wooden cross at their head which is painted black and bears the name of the person buried beneath.'

The work of throwing out the earth from Paole's grave was begun by the bent old sexton*. He seemed unconcerned enough but the drummer boy was gazing intently in horror and suspense at his activities. Before long the coffin was roughly dragged out of the ground, and the grave digger's assistant soon knocked off the lid. It was seen that the corpse had moved to one side, the jaws gaped wide open and the lips were moist with new blood which had trickled in a thin stream from the corner of the mouth. Unafraid, the sexton caught the body and twisted it straight.

"So," he cried, "You have not wiped your mouth since last night's work."

The surgeons, although used to the horrors of the battlefield, shrank back in disgust whilst the drummer boy fainted. Recovering their senses, the surgeons began to examine the body and concluded that Arnold Paole was indeed a vampire. The corpse still looked fresh, despite having been buried ten weeks previously. New skin had appeared under the old and the nails, too, had grown.

Having confirmed their worst fears, the party set about dealing with the vampire. Handfuls of garlic were scattered over the body. According to eyewitnesses, as the stake was driven through Arnold's body, a piercing shriek came from the corpse's lips and blood spouted from the wound.

Sexton: a church helper.

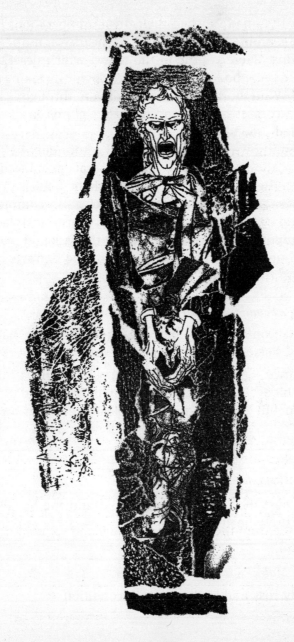

When they had finished their dreadful operation, the surgeons examined four other graves nearby and dug up their coffins. There is little in the report which describes the state of these bodies but they were obviously taking no chances. Whitethorn stakes were driven through each heart, the corpses burned and the ashes placed in newly consecrated ground.

This, sadly, was not the end of the torments of the villagers. About six years later several people died suddenly, the blood drained from their bodies. The authorities in Belgrade acted swiftly. A complete examination of all the bodies in the graveyard took place. Several important surgeons carried out the task and made some astonishing discoveries. The following extracts are taken from this medical report.

Stanna   *Female   Age 20   Dead for three months*

She had confessed on her deathbed that she had anointed herself with the blood of a vampire.

Appearance – untouched by decomposition. Chest full of fresh blood. The skin and nails of both hands and feet came off but underneath was a clean new skin and nails.

Miliza   *Female   Dead 100 days*

In the chest the blood was still liquid and the bowels were entirely healthy.

Miloc   *Male   Age 16   Dead 90 days*
The body rosy and in the vampire condition.

> **Unnamed young girl**   *Age 10   Dead 2 months*
> When pierced with a stake a great quantity of blood poured forth and swilled the grave.

All the bodies were removed from their graves and destroyed.

The report listed the 'living deaths' of many more vampires discovered in the graveyard. At the end of the report, the three distinguished army surgeons signed their names: Johannes Flickinger, Isaac Siedel, Johann Friedrich Baumgartner, countersigned by the remaining two officers. Having done their duty, they packed their bags and returned to Belgrade, satisfied that no more would be heard of vampirism – at least from the village of Meduegna.

Fang Files

Premature Burial

In the past it was not always easy to tell whether someone had really died. Even today, doctors do not always agree on when you can say someone is actually dead. There have been many examples of people who have appeared to have been dead and been mistakenly buried alive! Perhaps this had happened to Arnold Paole. Was he a case of premature burial? One thing is certain, however, the doctors made absolutely sure after they'd dug him up.

Testing for Death

To prevent premature burial, Egyptian priests kept bodies
under careful watch until they were satisfied they were
dead. The Greeks too were aware of the risk of premature
burial and tested corpses by cutting off fingers before
cremation or burial.

For thousands of years, there were other fairly simple tests for death. If there was no sign of you breathing then you had definitely died. In 1628, William Harvey, who discovered that the heart pumped blood around the body, added another rule. If the heart was not beating and there was no pulse then you were not likely to jump up and party.

Mistakes could Easily Happen

In 1746, Mr M. Cooper, a surgeon wrote, 'that many, apparently dead, have afterwards proved themselves alive by rising from their shrouds, their coffins and even their graves. I have seen this myself when a person of some distinction recovered when the priest was performing the funeral service over him in church. It is also certain that some persons, too quickly buried, have in their graves fallen victims to a death which might otherwise have been prevented' – in other words BURIED ALIVE!

The invention of the stethoscope* in 1816 made it easier for doctors to listen to heartbeats clearly. Since then a huge number of machines have been invented to test life activity in patients, such as brain scanners and electronic monitoring equipment. Even then some people have made amazing recoveries after being in deep comas and pronounced to be in a 'persistent vegatative state'. There have even been recent cases of people waking up in the mortuary!

Stethoscope: an instrument a doctor uses for listening to breathing.

Buried Alive – True Stories

Evidence of premature burial is difficult to obtain but not impossible. These fearful press cuttings speak for themselves.

The Lancet 17 March 1866
'Truly there is something about the very idea of being buried alive that sends a cold stream down one's spine. The rolling into the winding sheet, the screwing down of his coffin, the weeping at his funeral, and the final lowering of him into the narrow grave. Piling upon his dark and box-like dungeon loads of his mother earth. The last footfall departs from the lonely churchyard, leaving the sleeper behind in his hideous shell to awaken to a torment of activity. Screaming for help and clawing at the coffin lid until suffocation settles in to silence his protest. But it is soon past. There is scarcely room to turn over in the wooden chamber.'

The Lancet 12 September 1896
'A child of four years of age contracted typhoid fever and to every appearance had died. The time of the funeral was appointed and friends were on their way to attend. When the supposed corpse was about to be removed from the bed signs of life were noticed. The services of the medical man were again used and the child, rescued from a terrible death, is now making satisfactory progress.'

Some were not so lucky.

The London Echo 29 January 1901
'Some workmen, opening a vault at Ghent in Belgium yesterday, were horrified to discover the body of a young girl lying across the steps to true tomb. She was quite dead and had evidently been buried in a trance.'

Catalepsy

There are some people more likely to be buried alive than others, especially the sufferers of an illness called catalepsy. This usually strikes after the person has had a terrifying shock. All the muscles in the body suddenly lock rigid and the body's heartbeat and pulse are slowed down so much that they can barely be detected. Usually the attacks only last a few minutes but it has been known for the trance to last for several days. This can easily be mistaken for death.

The mother of General Lee, the famous American Civil War general, suffered from these death trances. On one occasion she was pronounced 'dead' and buried. Whilst the sexton was filling in the grave, however, he heard loud crying and knocking from inside the coffin. Mrs Lee was rescued from her horrible fate just in time!

A similar story is told of Lady Mount Edgcumbe who was laid to rest in the family vault after appearing dead. The sexton, who had noticed she was wearing a precious ring, returned in the dead of night to steal it. As he struggled to remove the valuable jewellery from her finger, she suddenly sat up. The man fled in terror, leaving the vault doors open. Having unexpectedly recovered from her rest, Lady Mount Edgcumbe walked to her house where she fainted into the arms of her husband.

In 1868, Herr Schwartz, an Indian missionary, was aroused from his supposed death by hearing his favourite hymn sung over him. The congregation suddenly became aware that he was alive when he joined in the singing!

One of the most remarkable cases was that of Colonel Townshend who possessed the power of 'voluntarily' dying. He could slow his heart down to such an extent that there was barely a pulse in his body. The longest period he remained in this state was about an hour and a half before active life slowly flowed back into his body.

Townshend lived before the invention of the stethoscope so that may explain why it was difficult to detect his heartbeat. Hibernating animals can also reduce their pulse from the normal 90 beats a minute to as few as eight or ten beats. When Colonel Townshend died in 1808, nine hours after one of his trances, a post-mortem was carried out on the body but no clues could be found as to his extraordinary power over his heart.

Indian holy men, known as *fakirs*, have stunning powers of control over their bodies. The *Medical Times*, 11 May 1850, reported the case of an Indian fakir who was buried alive under a couple of metres of earth and guarded closely. To make doubly sure there was no trickery, corn was sown over the 'grave'. During the time the man was buried it grew to a height of several centimetres. He lay there for 42 days. When the fakir was dug up his legs and arms were shrivelled and stiff but his face was full and healthy. No pulse could be discovered in the heart, temples, or arms but the man recovered fully in several hours.

Edgar Allan Poe, the famous horror writer, based a short story on a sufferer of catalepsy, called 'The Premature Burial'. The hero of the story suffers badly from the disease and has nightmares that he will mistakenly be thought to be dead and buried alive. He prepares his tomb so that he can escape should he suddenly awaken from his death-like trance. A long lever is installed so the slightest pressure will release the doors to the tomb, ventilation holes are made to admit the air and food placed in air-tight containers. The coffin lid is fitted with springs so that the slightest push from inside would release it. Suspended from the roof of the tomb is a large bell and rope to allow the victim to summon assistance. To find out what happens, however, you'll have to read Poe's story.

Narcolepsy

Narcolepsy is a less serious but no less mysterious condition in which sufferers experience sleeping trances. It has been well-known throughout history. Dr Madden who collected examples of this disease came across the case of a young man aged 25 in 1694, who slept for nearly a month. Two years later he again fell into a deep sleep and at first ate and drank without thinking but eventually ceased this altogether and continued to hibernate for 17 weeks. In August he fell asleep again and did not wake until November.

Marguerite Bozenval, the human 'dormouse' was even more remarkable. The Paris journalist of the *Morning Leader* reported her case on 1 February 1903. She had been in a trance for 20 years. In 1883, when she was 21, Bozenval had had an illegitimate child. Her friend told her that the police were coming to arrest her and she instantly fell into unconsciousness. Until a day or two before her death, she never woke from her sleep. Her mouth and eyes were always closed and she was fed through a tube placed in her mouth. The doctors needed to break a front tooth to fit it in. The first signs of life occurred when a doctor was treating an ulcer. She momentarily opened her eyes and asked after her grandfather who had died many years before. The effort to speak seemed more than she could bear and she died shortly afterwards.

If all this talk of being buried alive is making you feel a little uneasy then you might want to take a look at the invention of Count Karnice-Karnicki. The Count was a Russian nobleman and Doctor of Law. He was haunted by the story of the premature burial of a young Belgian girl. Standing by the graveside, he was horrified to hear the screams of the girl as she was aroused from her trance by the first shovelfuls of earth thumping upon her coffin.

He set himself the task of finding a simple solution to the problem. Here is his design. A long iron tube is fitted into the coffin. A glass ball is placed on the chest, attached to a spring which is connected through the iron tube to an iron box above ground. The box is normally closed to prevent gases escaping from the coffin above ground. On the slightest movement of the chest the glass ball releases a spring which causes the lid of the iron box to fly open, allowing air and light into the coffin. At the same time a flag is raised in the air. The pipe can also be used as a speaking tube.

All this was very reasonably priced at 12s – that's 60p to the likes of you and me!

Frightened to Death

The Strangest Case

In January 1973, Constable John Pye was patrolling the streets of Stoke-on-Trent. It was a bitter winter night and the slush beneath his feet had frozen to razor-sharp ridges of ice. He pulled his collar up tight and blew into his hands. He hated night shifts at the best of times; in winter it was unbearable. He momentarily thought of a steaming hot cup of tea at the police station, but this pleasant thought was interrupted by a call on his radio to investigate suspicious circumstances at a small terraced street nearby. It was to prove an investigation for which no amount of training could have prepared him.

He was met by the owner of No 3, 'The Villas'. The house had seen better times and was now split up into a number of one roomed flats.

"What's the problem, sir?"

The landlord hesitated for a moment. "I'm not sure. You see it's more a slight suspicion I have. I don't know. It's one of my tenants – Demetrious Myiciura. He's a Pole. Came over in '48. I thought I heard a choking sound. I've knocked but I can't get an answer. I didn't want to go in. He can be an awkward fella – very touchy about his privacy."

Constable Pye climbed the rickety stairs to the first landing and then paused outside Demetrious's door. Giving a short rap, he called out.

"Mr Myiciura. Are you there? Is everything all right?"

No answer.

Pye turned back to the landlord. "You're sure he's in there, are you? Couldn't have slipped out for something?"

"No, I'm sure. I'd have heard the tread on the stairs." Then, as an embarrassed afterthought, he added. "Some of the treads need fixing. Been waiting for the builder to come round. You know what they're like, always..."

Constable Pye cut him short. "Have you got a spare key to his room?"

A Vampire's Lair?

The landlord handed over a short, stubby key ingrained with dirt. The key turned in the lock and with a whining protest the door slowly opened. The room was in darkness. Pye groped around the door lintel until he came to the switch plate.

"Afraid of electricity he was," explained the landlord. "Believed it seeped out from the sockets. Even took out all the light bulbs."

Pye took out his pocket torch and directed the beam around the room. An astonishing sight met his eyes. Salt was scattered all around the room and over the blankets on the bed. As Pye followed the trail around the room, a dead man's face became etched in the torch beam. A bag of salt rested against his head and another was laid between his legs.

The young constable braced himself and went into the room. As he stepped into the gloom an overpowering smell of ammonia made his nostrils curl up in disgust. Pye could see that several small containers had been placed around the room. They were filled with the man's urine mixed with salt. On each wall, with the exception of the window wall, hung large crucifixes draped in garlic. Even the window ledge was covered in cloves of garlic.

Help was summoned and the room carefully examined. After notes had been made and photographs taken, the body was removed for examination. The pathologist noted that Myiciura appeared to have choked to death, discovering what he thought to be a large pickled onion wedged in the poor man's throat.

A Private Investigation

Meanwhile Constable Pye carried out further investigations of his own – at the local library. Undisturbed by the strange look from the librarian, he asked for books on vampires. One volume in particular held him in fascinated attention – Anthony Masters' *Natural History of the Vampire*. Within those pages, he began to piece together the bizarre circumstances of the Pole's death. Myiciura must have become terrified of becoming prey to vampires whom, he believed, rose from their graves at night to come to suck the blood from the living. Salt and garlic are traditional remedies for keeping vampires at a safe distance.

Armed with this information he explained his findings to the pathologist who was examining the corpse of Myiciura. Re-examining the 'pickled onion' they discovered that it was a large bulb of garlic. Presumably, Myiciura, in a last desperate attempt to protect himself against vampires, had slept with a clove of garlic in his mouth. And it was this that had killed him – his fear of vampires. So, in one sense, the 'undead' had claimed another victim.

The coroner was in no doubt as to the circumstances of the Pole's death. "This man genuinely believed in vampires and whilst he was obsessed by the subject I do not believe the man was clinically insane. Perhaps, his mind had been disturbed to some degree by the events he had experienced in his life. As a young man he had lost everything in the Second World War when the Germans invaded his country. His wife and children had been murdered and his farm taken from him. After the war he arrived in England penniless."

He continued, trying to offer an explanation for Myiciura's behaviour. "I've been a lawyer for a long time, dealing with all sorts of strange cases. I've seen all sorts of depravity, all sorts of nonsense, but I can understand what lay behind this man's thinking. A lot of evil had happened to him. Perhaps, for this unfortunate man, the evil was represented by vampires."

And there the coroner reached his verdict 'Death by misadventure'.

Who knows what had entered Myiciura's tortured mind? What is certain is that the consequences were fatal.

Fang Files

To most people vampire films are fun, but some people like Demetrious Myiciura take them DEADLY seriously. Hollywood has done much to spread and build upon the vampire legends.

The earliest vampire film to hit the silent screens came in 1912 and to date about 600 or more have been 'reeled-off' the production line from all corners of the world, including *Dracula* which had all the blood-dripping attraction to make film 'fan-gs' shiver in their seats. If you have time to sit through them all, some of the following masterpieces might make you scream or roll in the aisles with laughter...

In *Abbott and Costello Meet Frankenstein* (1949) Universal Film Studios pits its two famous comedians against Dracula, who is attempting to steal Costello's brain for Frankenstein's monster. In *Billy the Kid versus Dracula* (1966) the Kid has become a 'goody-goody' who kills the cloaked monster. Or maybe you'd like to sit through *Blood Beast Terror* (1969) and watch a giant, blood-sucking moth drain its human victims. If you feel a bit mushy, you might prefer *Blood Drinkers* (1966). In this film a vampire is bitten with the love bug and tries to save his dying girlfriend by kidnapping her twin sister to transplant her heart. Maybe your taste is for an 'all singing, all dancing' vampire movie. In which case you may want to sing along with *The Fearless Vampire Killers*; or *Pardon Me, but your Teeth are in My Neck* (1967). This was also released as *Dance of the Vampires* and was originally named for the dance sequence at the vampire's home.

And how about a couple of films for those who have 'green fingers' – well, before they get steeped in blood,

that is. *Little Shop of Horrors* (1960) tells the tale of a shop assistant at a florists that grows and feeds a plant that feeds off human blood. It was remade as *Please Don't Eat My Mother*. It later became a smash hit musical when it was made into a film under its original name. *Blood* (1973) has Dracula's plant-loving daughter and the Wolfman's son lovingly raising carnivorous plants in New York.

Are you hard of hearing? Then *Deafula* (1975) is the film for you, being shot entirely in sign language. Animal lovers will no doubt follow the trail of *Dracula's Dog* (1978). In this film the Transylvanian pooch heads for Los Angeles where he hopes to find a friendly master in the last surviving relative of Dracula.

If you'd like to find the most complete list of vampire films then have a look at:

The Illustrated Vampire Movie Guide Stephen Jones
Cinematic Vampire John L. Flynn

The 'Drac' Pack

Bela Lugosi 1882–1956

One of the earliest film stars who played Dracula was the actor Bela Lugosi who, strangely enough, was born in Hungary about 80 kilometres from Transylvania. Lugosi emigrated to America in 1920 and after playing Dracula on stage was given the film part. Dracula opened in 1931 to rave revues and became an immediate hit. Lugosi kept returning to his Dracula role, in between playing a variety of monsters and villains, including starring in the comedy film, *Abbot and Costello Meet Frankenstein*. Interest in horror films waned in the early 1950s and Bela found himself almost penniless. In 1956 he got the part in a vampire 'quickie' *Plan 9 from Outer Space*, but, sadly, a week after filming began, he died on 16 August 1956.

Christopher Lee 1922–

Christopher Lee is best known for his vampire roles, having appeared in more than 130 movies. The film that began it all was the *The Horror of Dracula* (1958) which became a spectacular success. The public thirsted for

more and several sequels followed in quick succession over the next seven years. He appeared in his last vampire movie in 1976 and has since played a variety of characters but he will always live in people's minds as 'the Count'.

Saved for the nation

Believe it or not – a £95,000 lottery grant has been given to keep Frankenstein's eyeballs and Dracula's fangs for the nation. Five hundred blood thirsty relics – werewolf hands, mummy masks from the famous film-makers, the Hammer House of Horrors, have been bought to go on display at the Bradford based Museum of Photography, Film and Television in Britain. Many were worn by the stars such as Christopher Lee in the heyday of the horror films in the 1950s and '60s.

Movie Madness

Watch out for the following films on TV if your parents will let you.

Count Dracula 1977 opens with the hero, Jonathan Harker saying goodbye to Lucy and her mother. He travels to Castle Dracula where he escapes from Count Dracula and his three female vampire residents who try to persuade him to stay longer – the rest of eternity! Returning to England, he finds that Lucy is engaged to a member of the American embassy in London, Dr John Steward. Dracula, however, has other ideas about the engagement and trails Jonathan to London, where he begins his attack on Lucy. Abraham Van Helsing, a professor, is called to the rescue and he explains the nature of the vampire attacks. Lucy finally dies but after several midnight hauntings. Jonathan and her family are persuaded to visit her tomb. In one of the most gruesome scenes in the movies, a stake is driven through Lucy's heart releasing a fountain of blood whilst she writhes in agony.

In the final scenes, Van Helsing and Mina (Lucy's sister) journey to Castle Dracula where, after the three female vampires are killed, Dracula's coffin lid is prised open, and the Count gets his just desserts – a large wooden stake through the heart.

The Addams Family

OK, so we all complain about our families at one time or another. But how would you feel about being a member of the Addams family?

The Addams family began life as a cartoon series in the *New Yorker* magazine in the 1930s. It was drawn by Charles S. Addams (1912–88).

In fact, Addams never gave names to his creepy-crawly family, so they were named when the television series was created in the 1960s. Mummy was called Morticia (she doused herself in embalming fluids to attract passing vampires). Gomez, her husband, was just a plain old boring 'undead'. Pugsley and Wednesday, their un-delightful children, Uncle Fester (the only true-blood, genuine vampire amongst them), Grandmama and the butler, Lurch, completed the household.

In 1991, the Addams family became movie stars in *The Addams Family*, followed by the sequel *Addams Family Values* in 1993. The family get into all sorts of weird adventures, turning all the things society believes are good and nice on their heads. Definitely a movie for all the family!

A Brief Tour of the World of Vampires

Legends of vampires occur throughout the world.

India

Many vampire legends originate in India. There is some evidence that these stories may have been brought to us by gypsies as they travelled westwards on their migration from India. In the ancient Hindu religion there are vampire-like creatures called Tal who were ogres and demons that lived in the cemeteries and who disrupted the lives of people who lived nearby. Amongst their many nasty practices they were held responsible for the killing of babies.

The *bhuta* are another type of Hindu demon that are believed to live near cremation grounds. These creatures were the souls of the dead who had committed suicide, or who had been insane. They wandered the night as dark shadows, flickering lights or misty spectres and could enter the bodies of corpses to enable them to stalk and gorge on living persons.

Africa

Of all the countries in the world, African countries have fewest beliefs in vampire mythology. One of the most famous is the *obafiyo*, the name given by the Ashanti people to a witch-like creature that lives secretly in their communities. This creature can leave its body and travel at night as a glowing ball of light. In this disguised state it attacks mainly children and sucks the blood from their bodies.

China

Chinese folklore tells of vampire-like creatures called *chiang-shi*. These demons were believed to be the inferior part of the soul that could linger in the body long after the person had died. Chiang-shi were incredibly strong in this condition, growing talons and claws to rip their victims to pieces. They were not normally recognised but if someone discovered their true nature then they gave off a green glow and were transformed into hideous, deformed shapes. Chiang-shi usually arose as the result of a violent death due to suicide, drowning, hanging or smothering.

Hope you've enjoyed the world trip so far. Time to make a last stop for a quick bite – Puerto Rico and the Chupacabras.

The New Vampire - the Chupacabras

The First Attacks

The first reports came in 1991. A ferocious killer was on the loose on the small island of Puerto Rico, over a thousand kilometres off the coast of Florida. The first victims were only goats, but even so the locals were terrified. The animals were found with teeth marks in their necks and drained of blood. Nothing like this had been seen before. The killer was given the nickname the 'Chupacabras', Spanish for the 'Goatsucker'.

Between March and August 1995 the attacks flared up again. Over 150 goats were slaughtered around Cananovas. By December the problem was far worse. The killing had spread throughout Puerto Rico and the Chupacabras had started to vary its diet. During 1996 thousands of birds, sheep and cattle, as well as goats, were found dead. Ismael Aponte, the Director of Civil Defence for Cananovas told reporters:

"When the Goatsucker attacks it leaves perfect incisions, two round marks in the neck. It sucks out the blood and liver of every single animal."

Puerto Rican journalist Eddie Deese noticed another pattern to the crimes:

"Most attacks by the Chupacabras are near water, a stream, a creek or a river bed. He digs holes, but no one knows why he digs them."

It was little wonder that many villagers feared that a new vampire-like creature was on the loose. In the rainforest area of El Yunque they began to build strong shelters to protect their animals. Chemo Soto, Mayor of Cananovas, grimly commented:

"People in the village are hysterical and very scared. They won't go out in the street after dark. They are terrified that the Chupacabras will attack them."

A Devil on the Loose

As panic spread the beast was sighted more often. Luciano Guadalupe was stunned by what he saw:

"We went outside and the Chupacabras was on some scaffolding, crouched as if it was going to spring. Then it jumped off and flew away. It had huge wings."

Some witnesses saw the Chupacabras standing on two feet, others on all fours. A few people claimed it had wings, others three long claws. Most agreed that it was the size of a human, about two metres tall. Ismael Aponte listened to dozens of stories and found notable similarities. He put together this fearsome description: "It looks like a kangaroo. It has a snout like a pig and huge slit eyes, big pointed ears and feet like a kangaroo, but it's fast and strong in a way that a kangaroo isn't."

American investigator Bob Schott came to Puerto Rico in the hope of tracking down the Goatsucker. In April 1996 he visited a ranch near Cananovas just after a raid by the Chupacabras. This time two sheep had been attacked, one had died but the other had survived. Schott was shocked to see that its tail had been ripped out. Whatever had done this had tremendous strength.

The army was called in to hunt the Goatsucker down and an investigation launched. What was it and could it be killed? Experts were puzzled. There were no large wild mammals on Puerto Rico, so it was not likely that villagers were mistakenly reporting big cats, like panthers or

pumas. In any case the tooth bites in the victims were far deeper than those of any known animal. Even creepier were the three clawed foot prints found near the deaths. Just like the bites, they couldn't be identified.

A lucky break led to a blood sample. A policeman shot and winged what he believed was the Chupacabras as it leapt a fence. Blood stains were found and analysed but only added to the mystery. It was not a match for any human or animal blood yet known to science.

An Unsolved Mystery

So what is the Chupacabras? Aponte has a frightening theory:

"This was a genetic experiment involving various animals and the Goatsucker was the outcome. Possibly it comes from an American military base on the island."

Schott, too, thinks the US government knows what is going on but is keeping quiet.

A second theory claims that the Chupacabras is a being from another world. Puerto Rico is also a hot spot for UFO sightings, so perhaps the Goatsucker is an alien investigating Earth. If this is so, there have been several landings. In 1997 the Chupacabras was also spotted in Mexico, the USA and Spain.

Eddie Deese has the same worry as many Puerto Ricans. How long before the Goatsucker gets tired of goat's blood and begins to prey on humans? If it does Aponte says he is ready:

"After so long hunting the Chupacabras, so many sleepless nights, so many headaches, so much fatigue, if I meet up with him either he'll get me or I'll get him."

Fang Files

Mysterious, vampire-like killings are not only found in Puerto Rico. There have been reports of them from all over the world for many years. In the cases you are about to read no culprit, human or supernatural has ever been caught. But perhaps there are lessons that may explain what has been happening on Puerto Rico.

The Irish Sheep Killer

In 1874 there was an outbreak of sheep killing near Cavan in Ireland. Forty-two animals were found dead with their throats cut and their blood drained. Yet no flesh had been eaten. Outraged farmers, armed with guns, searched the area for a culprit and several dogs were shot. Then reports came in of another rash of sheep slaughter around Limerick, 160 kilometres away. Both incidents stopped of their own accord and no clear answer was ever found. Was this the great-grandfather of the Chupacabras?

English Chicken Slaughter

In January 1905 more than 200 chickens were killed over several nights at Binbrook Farm, near Market Rasen, England. The slaughter happened even when the farmer stood guard outside the henhouse. Creepily the chickens all died in the same way – the skin was ripped from around their necks and their windpipes snapped.

The Tragedy of Snippy the Horse

Snippy was a three-year-old gelding, the beloved pet of American couple, Mr and Mrs Berle Lewis. (Actually Snippy was a mare called Lady, but poor reporting at the time has always led to this being known as the Snippy story.) He was pastured in a remote ranch in Colorado's San Luis Valley. Snippy was last seen frisking happily near the ranch house at dusk on 7 September 1967. The next day his body was discovered in a pasture half a kilometre away. His head and neck had been stripped of skin, his blood drained and several internal organs had been removed. Cuts on the carcass were said to have been done with 'surgical precision'.

In the years that followed thousands of animals, especially cattle, were found dead across the USA and Canada. One study claimed that as many as 10,000 had been attacked between 1973 and 1979. Often they had the same surgical cuts, drained blood and missing body parts as Snippy. As panic spread worried ranchers listened to wild theories. Some experts blamed vampires or devil worshippers, others suggested secret government experiments or UFOs.

In 1979, like an episode from the *X-Files*, the FBI investigated. The job was given to a top, retired agent Kenneth Rommel. After a years work his report *Operation Animal Mutilation* was delivered to the District Attorney at Sante Fe. Rommel wrote that nothing weird or alien was happening, and that the damage done to the dead animals was natural.

Some of the injuries were caused when the bodies started to rot, the 'missing' blood for example simply drained to the bottom of the carcass, coagulating (thickening) and drying out. Even the fearfully precise surgical cuts were just the marks left by scavengers picking at the corpse. Coyotes for instance have teeth that can shear flesh so neatly that only a microscope can show the difference between the work of their razor-sharp incisors and a scalpel. Blow flies nibbling at dead flesh can tidy up the rough edges so that they seem surgically neat.

Yet the truth is often boring and many people choose to believe that Rommel was only one more part of a sinister government cover-up. Certainly TV Agents Mulder and Scully wouldn't go along with Agent Rommel's common sense approach.

Animal Vampires

Bats

Bram Stoker didn't do bats any favours when he wrote *Dracula*. In the novel the evil Count changed into bat form several times. His first victim in London, Lucy Westrana, noted in her diary:

17 September. Night.
I was waked by the flapping at the window, which had begun after that sleep walking on the cliff at Whitby when Mina saved me and which I now know so well… Then outside in the shrubbery I heard a sort of howl like a dog, but more fierce and deeper. I went to the window and looked out, but could see nothing but a big bat, which had evidently been buffeting its wings against the window.

Bats have become a common image in horror movies, up there amongst the top ten creepies with spiders and snakes. But do they deserve this reputation?

There are over 1000 different species of bats and they are the only mammals that can fly. Bats have a relaxed lifestyle and spend most of their time hanging upside down and sleeping. Some species are virtually blind and find their way around with an amazing echo location system, bouncing high pitched squeaks off solid objects and listening for the echo. Most, however, have good night vision, so unlike birds they can fly in the dark and prefer to hunt after dusk.

In Europe they live in old buildings like church towers or steeples and are often seen flitting around graveyards. This may seem creepy to some nervous humans but it's common sense for bats. Graveyards are green open spaces, rich in bat snacks – not dead bodies, but insects.

Vampire Bats

Vampire bats were so called by the great Spanish conqueror, Cortés. Whilst he was destroying the Aztec Empire in Mexico in 1520 his troops came across blood sucking bats. Cortés remembered European vampire legends and gave these strange creatures their chilling name.

There are three species of vampire bats but they only live in Central and South America. Two species feed on birds but *Desmodus rotundus*, the common vampire bat feeds on mammals. They find the blood of grazing animals, like cattle, especially tasty. They are also wonderfully agile and can walk, run, hop and turn somersaults, as well as fly. Their sense of smell is excellent and their large eyes give them clear night vision.

When vampire bats attack they are sneaky. They walk quietly over to a sleeping victim and, make a small wound with razor-sharp incisor teeth. This is usually painless and doesn't disturb the prey. They choose their spot carefully, a part of the body rich in small blood vessels such as the tip of the nose, ears, eyelids or lips. When the blood starts to flow, they don't suck like Dracula, but lap like a cat drinking milk. Their saliva has an anticoagulant, a substance to keep the blood flowing while they feed.

Vampire bats weigh about 30 grams and if they are hungry they can drink more than their weight in blood. After feeding they are so heavy they have to wait for their meal to digest before they can take off. Human blood donors usually give a pint of their own blood to hospitals, this would be enough to feed a vampire bat for at least a month.

Usually vampire bats don't attack humans, but if they are hungry and nothing tastier is around then they make the best of it. The Victorian explorer Charles Waterton described a raid on his friend:

> On examining his foot, I found the vampire had tapped his great toe: there was a wound somewhat less than that made by a leech; the blood was still oozing from it. Whilst examining it, I think I put him in a worse mood by remarking that a European surgeon would not have been so generous as to blood him without making a charge.

Waterton continues wistfully,

> I had often wished to have been sucked by a vampire…There can be no pain in the operation as the patient is always asleep when the vampire is sucking; and as for the loss of a few ounces of blood, that would be a trifle in the long run. Many a night have I slept with my foot out of the hammock to tempt this winged surgeon, expecting he would be there; but it was all in vain.

The Case against Vampire Bats

M'lud. The case for the prosecution:

Although vampire bats don't drink much blood, the anticoagulants they use mean the blood of their victims keeps flowing after they have stopped feeding. If several bats feed off the same cow, it can be left weak. Far worse they carry rabies, a deadly disease, and transmit it to their prey. They have been known to attack humans, including babies. It is safer to wipe them out by gassing the caves they live in.

The Case for Vampire Bats

M'lud, the case for the defence:

Vampire bats are sweet and cuddly. They share their food, groom and care for each other. They are the only hunters that do not kill their prey. Most cattle would prefer to be attacked by a vampire bat than a wild cat or dog. There is little evidence to show that wiping out the bats cuts the spread of rabies.

Vampire Bats 0 – British Children Won!

Inspite of their fearsome reputation, vampire bats are nervous creatures. The first six to arrive in Britain were sent from an American university in 1964. Shortly after they were shown to pupils in a Basingstoke school they all, sadly, died. The shock of meeting the children was too much for them.

Really Vicious Vampires

The world's worst bloodsuckers are the smallest – insects. Parasitic insects live off the blood of their prey. Those that feed on humans include mosquitoes, horse-flies, midges, blackflies, fleas, lice and bed bugs. Some, like mosquitoes, only visit people for a meal, others, like fleas, live happily on the bodies of their hosts.

The sharp nose, or proboscis, of the mosquito is designed for attack. Six different tubes have specialised jobs – cutting a hole in the skin; injecting anticoagulant; injecting digestive juices and sucking blood out. Have you heard the saying *The female of the species is deadlier than the male*? Mosquitoes prove it. Mummy mosquito is the vicious one, she needs blood to help her eggs mature. Males either don't feed at all or just sip a little nectar.

> 'Nite nite,
> Sleep tight,
> Don't let the bed bugs bite.'

Have you heard this old Victorian ditty? Around 1900, three out of four homes were infested with bed bugs. The tiny terrors were knocked out by the pesticide DDT in the 1940s but now they are back for revenge. A new breed of bed bugs resistant to any treatment is on the loose and hungry. And be careful what your family buys at car boot and garage sales, bed bugs are often carried from house to house in second-hand furniture.

Like Dracula, bed bugs feed on human blood and usually attack their victims as they sleep. The 0.5 cm black pests suck as much as four times their own unfed body weight in blood. Their feeding frenzy lasts up to 15 minutes and leaves victims covered in itchy, red bumps.

Now you've almost finished this blood curdling book it might be time for a bedroom bed bug hunt, but you'll need a very small splinter to stake these creatures of the night...

The Last Bite

Recovered your senses? Feeling drained after reading so many blood-dripping tales? If you're afraid to venture out of doors then don't worry for help is at hand. Look for the clues in these pictures to see if your neighbourhood is going batty!

Index

Truly Terrible Tales

Scientists
Writers
Explorers
Inventors

Jack Marlowe
illustrated by Scoular Anderson

History is crammed with amazing stories!
In these four books you can find out all about the
terrible but true lives of famous scientists, writers,
explorers and inventors through the ages:

Creepy John Dee, Tudor scientist – or wicked
magican?

Roman horror king Seneca, whose own death was
as nasty as his bloodthirsty plays ...

Fearless Florence Baker, Victorian explorer, who
saw her own grave being dug ...

And Ancient Greek Arcimedes, creator of the
deadly ship-smasher!

Order Form

0 340 73992 4	Truly Monstrous Tales: **Vampires**	£3.99	☐
0 340 73993 2	Truly Monstrous Tales: **Werewolves**	£3.99	☐
0 340 73994 0	Truly Monstrous Tales: **Mummies**	£3.99	☐

All Hodder Children's books are available at your local bookshop or newsagent, or can be ordered direct from the publisher. Just tick the titles you want and fill in the form below. Prices and availability subject to change without notice.

Hodder Children's Books, Cash Sales Department, Bookpoint, 39 Milton Park, Abingdon, Oxon, OX14 4TD, UK. If you have a credit card you may order by telephone – (01235) 400414.

Please enclose a cheque or postal order made payable to Bookpoint Ltd to the value of the cover price and allow the following for postage and packing:

UK & BFPO – £1.00 for the first book, 50p for the second book, and 30p for each additional book ordered, up to a maximum charge of £3.00.

OVERSEAS & EIRE – £2.00 for the first book, £1.00 for the second book, and 50p for each additional book.

Name ....

Address ....

....

....

If you would prefer to pay by credit card, please complete the following:

Please debit my Visa/Access/Diner's Card/American Express (delete as applicable) card no:

----- ----- ----- ----- ----- ----- ----- ----- ----- ----- ----- ----- ----- ----- ----- -----

Signature ....

Expiry Date ....